Meditations and Visualizations

for writers and aspiring authors

Joanne Fedler

Illustrated by Margaret Rolla

Cover illustration *Writer's Journey* Watercolour and digital montage [297 X 210mm]

Copyright 2019 by Joanne Fedler
First published by Joanne Fedler Media, 2019.
www.joannefedler.com

Illustrations and design by Margaret Rolla
www.margaretrolla.com.au

All rights reserved. No part of this publication may be reproduced, stored in a retrieval system or transmitted in any form or by any means, electronic, mechanical photocopying, recording or otherwise without the prior written permission of the author.

Printed in Australia, UK and USA.

National Library of Australia Cataloguing-in-Publication data:

ISBN: 978-1-925842-19-7 (Paperback)
ISBN: 978-1-925842-20-3 (Ebook)

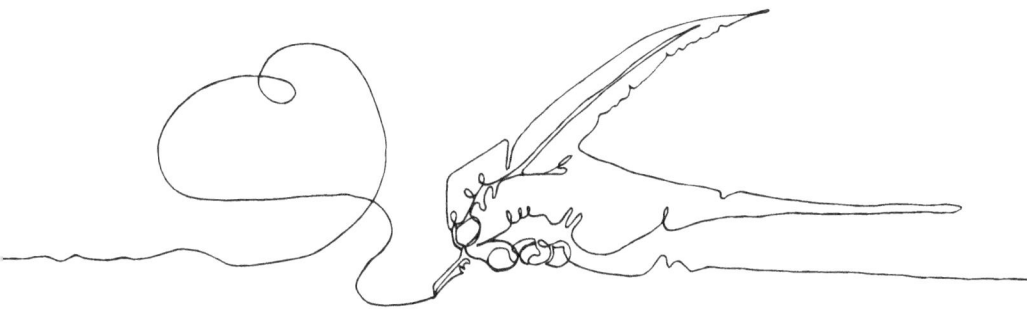

Contents

Page	Chapters
6	Introduction
10	Meditation 01: Commencement
14	Meditation 02: Conviction
18	Meditation 03: Curiosity
22	Meditation 04: Conscientiousness
26	Meditation 05: Conscientiousness
30	Meditation 06: Courage
34	Meditation 07: Connection
38	Meditation 08: Commitment
44	Meditation 09: Chutzpah

Introduction

Introduction

In 2001, I was in a writing group trying to finish the first draft of my first book, *The Dreamcloth*. I knew I wanted to be an author. But still, I lacked the self-assurance that what I'd written was good enough to be published. At times, my self-doubt felt like a form of self-sabotage—a shrinkage from the one true accomplishment that would make my life meaningful to me.

In the spirit of mentoring my uncertain self, I wrote on a small card, *I AM A WRITER*. I laminated it. And on the back, I wrote, *Don't forget the book and the magic it carries. You can do it.*

I tacked this card up on my computer screen with adhesive. Each day when I sat down to write, *I AM A WRITER* winked at me. Those impossible words, by stealth and seepage, became a prophecy I would fulfil many times over in years to come.

***

What do writers need?

Besides time, a room of one's own and some knowledge of the craft of writing, what supports aspiring writers to become authors?

I've spent years angling for the answer to this question by mentoring hundreds of writers, running writing retreats, developing online writing courses and authoring ten books of my own.

My hope is that this little book offers a solution.

***

Every book begins with a dream.

If you can imagine it, you can create it.

MEDITATIONS AND VISUALIZATIONS

The great German poet and philosopher Rilke wrote, "The future enters us long before it happens." And so it is.

The greatest sportspeople visualize their goals before they tackle them. I create visionboards for each book before I write it. The brain, according to those who know a great deal about that filigreed nest of wires, cannot tell the difference between an imagined and an actual event. How powerful then, is the process of giving ourselves a story, rich with symbolism and metaphor, as a primer to which our writing can adhere?

> meditation ...an appetizer to the soul as we cast the net of our dreams

In teaching others how to write, I use visualization and meditation to allow the mind to experience the intended outcome before it materializes. It's an appetizer to the soul as we cast the net of our dreams a few feet ahead of us, and then simply follow the trail we have already traversed in our imagination.

Writing is a form of conception. I've witnessed many aspiring authors get stuck on the craft of writing, forgetting that creativity is fed by more than just know-how. Writing, like all art, is a blend of both craft and what I call 'consciousness.' It draws breath from all things, including emptiness, chaos, quiet, dreaming and visualization. Over the past decade, I've developed an approach to teaching writing based on qualities of consciousness which activate creativity:

Commencement • Conviction • Curiosity • Conscientiousness Courage • Connection • Commitment • Chutzpah

Introduction

My hope is that these meditations and visualizations support you during your writing journey, as you navigate the treacheries of self-doubt, resistance, fear, envy, uncertainty, irrelevance, impatience, lack of originality, entrapment in cliché and that ever-corrupting virus of a question: "Who am I to write this book?"

These meditations are accompanied by beautiful original artwork by the astonishingly talented Marg Rolla. I am indebted to her for adding a new dimension to these meditations, expanding the morphic field and metaphoric radiance of these spirit stories.

How to Use This Book

- Work through one meditation a day—read it aloud to yourself. Then sit with it. What feelings does it evoke in you? Write them down.

- Identify where you are struggling in your writing and then read the corresponding meditation as medicine.

- Remember how as a child, you could get lost inside an illustration? Let yourself fall into the image and then reflect on how it relates to your writing journey.

...all you
need to
do is take
this first
step

01

Commencement

WHEN TO USE THIS MEDITATION

When you're struggling to give yourself permission to write, when you don't know how or where to begin, or when you feel overwhelmed at the task ahead.

Dorothy 26.5 X 35.5cm [watercolour and gouache]

Meditation

Close your eyes. Feel your body resting against the back of your chair, your feet firmly on the ground, your hands gently resting in your lap.

Take a few deep grounding breaths. Feel the air fill your lungs and gently exhale.

Take another breath and feel the fresh oxygen bringing life to every cell in your body. As you exhale, let go of everything you do not need to hold on to anymore.

Take a couple more deep grounding breaths.

Now imagine that you are about to undertake a new journey. You are standing at the edge of a forest looking into its vastness.

You are about to embark on a journey into the unfamiliar, into new territory.

Stop for a moment and feel what it's like to hold the energy of beginnings. Feel what it is like to take the first new steps into the unknown.

As you look into the forest and you anticipate what lies ahead, you can only see the first few steps in front of you and then the path disappears amongst the trees. And as you feel this moment of anticipation, tinged maybe with anxiety about the unknown and what it holds, and whether you're up to the task and what dangers might lie ahead, I want you to return into your body, and remember how many times you have begun anew. How many beginnings you have had.

Commencement

Many years ago, you once took your first breath. You may not remember it, but your body does.

Every part of you knew how to take its first breath.

You may not remember it, but you also took your first steps. You found your balance even though you faltered, even though you fell. You always got back up again. You kept going. And now you don't even think about breathing or walking. They are part of you. But once upon a time, you were just beginning to breathe, just beginning to walk.

You also learned to speak. You learned one word at a time. And now, you have language, and it's with this great resource inside you that you now begin this new journey of writing.

Trust that inside of you, everything exists to ensure you can begin this journey with everything inside you that you need to undertake it.

All you need to do is take this first step.

Trust your feet to take you where they need to go. Feel your feet now. Wriggle them, those trusty animals. They have brought you to this moment. Feel your hands resting in your lap. Those trusty friends. Now, feel your heart beating in your ribcage, a treasure chest of first times—first loves, first heartbreaks, first losses. It has known so many beginnings, and it never gives up. This beginning is just another one.

Take a few more grounding breaths. Rest your hands on your heart, one on top of the other. Feel the power inside you.

Open your eyes. You are ready to begin.

...your heart tells you which path you should take and you follow it

02

Conviction

WHEN TO USE THIS MEDITATION

When you're struggling with self-doubt, perfectionism, envy, fear of being judged and anxiety about what people will say.

Crossroads 21.5 X 28.5cm [watercolour]

Meditation

Close your eyes. Feel your body resting against the back of your chair, your feet firmly on the ground, your hands gently resting in your lap.

Take a few deep grounding breaths. Feel the air fill your lungs and gently exhale.

Take another breath and feel the fresh oxygen bringing life to every cell in your body. As you exhale, let go of everything you do not need to hold on to anymore.

Take a couple more deep grounding breaths.

Feel your spine holding you up, supporting you, this bony architecture that allows you to stand, to be upright, to move, to walk, to take steps. Feel now how much power and energy your body holds.

Now imagine you have taken your first few steps into the forest you were contemplating entering. You have ventured quite a way in, and you can no longer see where you entered. Ahead of you it is dark, the foliage is thick and you cannot see very far ahead. With every step you take, you must consider. Will I go this way, or that way?

You know that there is no one here to guide you but yourself. No one to ask: "Is this right?" "Am I making a mistake?" "Which is the best route?"

Now you come to a fork in the path and you must decide. You must choose: "Will I go left or will I go right?" You move towards the left and as you take that path, you suddenly feel your heart beating—perhaps this is not the right way. You turn back and you take the path that goes right but again, after a few steps, you second-guess yourself.

Now you are totally confused. You turn back and you stand at the crossroads. You close your eyes.

You take a few deep grounding breaths. You feel your spine holding you solid and your feet firmly on the ground. You listen to the sounds of the forest.

Inside of you, a small voices asks, "Who'm I to be journeying alone into this dark forest? Who'm I?" You feel lost and unsure.

But the small voice inside you flickers, and then quietens like a dying ember.

You pause, you stand firm. And suddenly, you sense something new glimmer inside you, a new energy. You feel the air around you, and it is charged with quiet certainty. Your heart tells you which path you should take and you follow it, knowing it will not lead you astray. You trust the forest, you trust the ground beneath your feet and you trust yourself that you will not, you cannot get lost.

You know there is something waiting for you inside this forest that you have come to retrieve, and that you must journey there. It is part of your life's mission.

Each time you exhale, you're relaxing, softening, and letting go of anything that can hold you back or stop you from writing. Let all the anxiety dissolve away from you. And feel your conviction getting stronger and stronger. And so you take a deep breath and you take your next steps, choosing the path that feels right to you. And as you choose, you feel equipped. You are ready, you're excited, you're supported and you feel guided.

The Guide 21 X 28.5cm [watercolour and gel pen]

...the light guides you as you delve deeper and deeper

03

WHEN TO USE THIS MEDITATION

When you're struggling with cliché, boredom, being boring, fear of being boring and have lost your sense of why you're writing and what makes your writing unique and interesting.

Meditation

Close your eyes. Feel your body resting against the back of your chair, your feet firmly on the ground, your hands gently resting in your lap.

Take a few deep grounding breaths. Feel the air fill your lungs and gently exhale.

Take another breath and feel the fresh oxygen bringing life to every cell in your body. As you exhale, let go of everything you do not need to hold on to anymore.

Take a couple more deep grounding breaths.

You are back in the forest.

You know now that you are your own guide on this journey. So you keep moving through the forest. You hear movement up ahead and for a moment, you are afraid. What if it is something dangerous? What if it is something that could harm you?

But then you remember that you have chosen this path, and nothing you have chosen is a mistake.

As you push through the trees, you see a figure walking towards you. Who is it? What are they doing in the forest?

You feel yourself full of questions and wonder. The figure doesn't come directly towards you, but makes its own way, and you start to follow it, not with fear, but with genuine curiosity. Where is it going? What language does it speak?

Every time you feel you are getting closer, the figure seems to move further and further away from you. Now you are following in its footsteps. And your mind is filled with all the questions you have for this person.

You call out into the shadows, "Hello, who are you?"

But the figure just quietly moves through the forest. It is, you sense, a benevolent presence. One that knows you, that has almost been expecting you.

The figure you follow starts to radiate light, and the light guides you as you delve deeper and deeper into the forest. Even though you do not know anything about this figure, you trust that it is taking you where you need to go, you with all your questions.

Every now and then, the figure drops something for you, and you pick it up—you don't know what some of these objects are—they seem random and unconnected, a stone, a sealed envelope, a pair of scissors, but you collect them as you follow.

"Who are you?" you shout out. "Who are you?"

And then you hear the echo coming back to you. "Who are you? Who are you?"

And you stop, and you wonder, "Who am I?"

And as you ask this question, you feel lit up inside.

You take the question "WHO AM I?" and you breathe it into your heart. You feel every single one of your senses tinglingly alert. Your heart feels bright and light in your chest. You feel alive, present and awake.

You take a few more deep breaths and you keep moving steadily forward into the welcoming darkness of the forest.

...how
that
energy
flows
out of
you
in the
words
you
write

04

Conscientiousness

WHEN TO USE THIS MEDITATION

When you're struggling with the labour of the craft, the structure of your writing or aspects of the process that must be learned (with no shortcut).

Elements 28.5 X 37cm [watercolour and gouache]

Meditation

Close your eyes. Feel your body resting against the back of your chair, your feet firmly on the ground, your hands gently resting in your lap.

Take a few deep grounding breaths. Feel the air fill your lungs and gently exhale.

Take another breath and feel the fresh oxygen bringing life to every cell in your body. As you exhale, let go of everything you do not need to hold on to anymore.

Take a couple more deep grounding breaths.

Settle into your body.

Feel the swirl of ideas and information that you've been gathering. Picture the storm spinning around you—character, setting, structure, plot, point of view. In the center of this whirlwind, you are standing completely still, completely centered.

As you take a few deep breaths, you radiate a sense of calm. And as you do, the storm of ideas begins to settle like a light drizzle, and it falls onto your skin and sinks into your body. You feel the cool tickle of these ideas as you absorb them completely.

Now everything around you is calm and peaceful.

Ahead, you see a circle of light where the trees part. And as you walk towards it, you understand that you need to bring the energy you need to create your book into this circle. Do you want the energy of flow, of emotion, of water? Do you want the fire energy of passion, stimulation and excitement? Or do you need stones and rocks for the earthy groundedness of reality?

Now see yourself gathering your elements of choice—whether it's mud, earth, stones, water, fire, feathers, leaves. Now build your circle of energy.

Once you've done that, see yourself standing in the center of this powerful circle that embodies your writing and the energy it will bring into the world. Allow yourself to be surrounded by it. See how that energy flows out of you in the words you write.

You are the creator of your life, your dreams and your writing. Everything you do from hereon in is filled with this energy, even as it touches the hearts and souls of the people who are going to read your book.

Take some deep breaths. Every time you inhale, the energy gets stronger and clearer.

Feel how the elements support you, how benevolent the universe is to your desires. How close you are to truly living in a way that is powerfully, uniquely your own.

Chorus of Creation 22 X 28.5cm [watercolour]

...to experience the beauty, richness and order of all things

05

Conscientiousness

WHEN TO USE THIS MEDITATION

When you need to connect with a place in your writing and to ground it in landscape (time, place, history, social events, politics), when you're battling with structure, theme and patterning and when you need to know and understand the "how" of your writing.

Meditation

Close your eyes. Feel your body resting against the back of your chair, your feet firmly on the ground, your hands gently resting in your lap.

Take a few deep grounding breaths. Feel the air fill your lungs and gently exhale.

Take another breath and feel the fresh oxygen bringing life to every cell in your body. As you exhale, let go of everything you do not need to hold on to anymore.

Take a couple more deep grounding breaths.

Settle into your body.

You have been walking a long way, through many different terrains. Sometimes you have wondered, "Is there a shortcut?" But by now you have embraced the full knowledge that the path you are on is the one you are meant to be on. You are not in a rush to "get anywhere" anymore. You start to slow down.

Now you take off your shoes and feel your feet on the earth. You take each step with full attention to how the warm earth feels underfoot. You savour each footstep, knowing it is taking you to where you need to go.

As you walk, you feel how you are held from beneath by the earth, and from above by the sky overhead. You imbibe the setting around you—the sentry of trees, the sounds of the wildlife hidden in the brush, the wind, the sun, the water that moves deep beneath the ground in a silent water table.

Conscientiousness

Clouds gather above and block out the sun, but then move on. You feel the pulse of the trees around you as they take in carbon dioxide and by a generous alchemy of their unseen metabolism, release oxygen back into the air for you to breathe.

You see a leaf fall from a tree, and you bend to pick it up. You hold it in your hand and as you examine it, you see its veins radiating from a central spine to the outer edges of the leaf.

And suddenly you sense it, the invisible order, the beautiful inner music of the leaf, the tree, the earth, the sky and you. You bow your head in humility and thanks for being part of such a sacred pattern, knowing that the perfection is in the detail—in the dust beneath your feet, and the rain that falls from the sky. You sense how every leaf and every creature in this forest is performing its part in the hidden architecture of your journey. The sun gives you daylight to carry on with your journey, and the night gives you sanctuary to rest.

Take a moment now to feel the ebb and flow of life, to experience the beauty, richness and order of all things, and how you too are part of this.

And you feel it in your heart, how you are related to it all, and you can learn from it all. And that no detail is in vain, no musical note out of order.

You see divine presence in each detail and begin to understand that nothing is here by accident. Nothing you do is a "mistake." You are learning that everything is unfolding around you in perfect harmony.

You sink to your knees and place your forehead on the ground in a gesture of sublime humility. You give thanks for the many teachers your path has placed in front of you and the chance you have to play your part in the chorus of creation.

...let the
light that
shines in
you flow
into your
writing
and
into the
world

06

Courage

WHEN TO USE THIS MEDITATION

When you're struggling with fear, when your writing is too painful and you feel vulnerable and when you know you need to take a risk with your writing.

Completeness 21.5 X 28.5cm [watercolour, digital]

MEDITATIONS AND VISUALIZATIONS

Close your eyes. Feel your body resting against the back of your chair, your feet firmly on the ground, your hands gently resting in your lap.

Take a few deep grounding breaths. Feel the air fill your lungs and gently exhale.

Take another breath and feel the fresh oxygen bringing life to every cell in your body As you exhale, let go of everything you do not need to hold on to anymore.

Take a couple more deep grounding breaths.

Settle into your body.

You keep walking on your path, and soon you come to a little clearing, where you see a young girl playing at the side of a pond. She is singing to herself and making things from the sticks and the leaves and the flowers in the forest. And you stop and you watch her for a little while. She is so uninhibited, so creative, so joyful.

She looks up and smiles at you.

Next to her is an old woman watching over her. As you approach them, the old woman looks into your eyes, and you see kindness, intelligence, sensitivity, suffering, grief, joy—you see her whole life in her eyes.

And as you stand there, looking into the eyes of this innocent, joyful, creative, beautiful child, you feel her melting into your body.

And from behind, you feel the old woman's presence, and you turn and she embraces you and melts into you.

As you, the old woman and the little girl become one, you feel a sense of completeness.

Now take a few deep breaths and feel how wonderful it is to have your inner child and your wise self integrated into your being. Feel how whole and gathered you feel. You have your history and your future self as your guides. And you now feel how powerful and strong you are, how you have everything inside you to write your book.

Picture yourself holding your book in your hands, filling up your belly, heart, soul, mind. And feel how different you feel knowing that this is something you can do, that you know how to do it, that it's not a mountain too hard or too high to climb. See the way your book is received, and touches, and changes people's lives.

And you know that even if you get overwhelmed or frustrated, you will know how to find your way back, without judgement and condemnation.

You will look after yourself lovingly the way a grandmother might comfort a child having a tantrum or who is frustrated. You recognize and acknowledge, it's okay to need help. It's okay not to know. You know you are not alone. You know that if you need to take a break, you can; if you need to ask questions, you can; if you don't know what to do, you have someone to ask. You will work it out.

Just take a moment to acknowledge what an enormous act of self-love it is for you to take this on, to write your book and put it out into the world.

You are here to share your story. To let the light that shines in you flow into your writing and into the world.

...your singing breaks the silence and the stars gather closer in to listen to your stories

07

Connection

WHEN TO USE THIS MEDITATION

When you're struggling to connect with your writing or a character in your story, when you're feeling lost and disconnected from your story and when you're struggling to make the connection between the personal and the universal in your writing.

Meditation

Close your eyes. Feel your body resting against the back of your chair, your feet firmly on the ground, your hands gently resting in your lap.

Take a few deep grounding breaths. Feel the air fill your lungs and gently exhale.

Take another breath and feel the fresh oxygen bringing life to every cell in your body. As you exhale, let go of everything you do not need to hold on to anymore.

Take a couple more deep grounding breaths.

Settle into your body.

You are deep in the heart of the forest. You can't seem to find a path anywhere. Everywhere you look, there are only trees. But though you do not know where you are, you are not afraid. You know you are safe.

It is starting to get dark.

It is quiet and the night is gathering around you.

But you know what to do. You know that your body is your home, that your heart is your refuge. You stand still. You feel the earth beneath you. You feel your strong skeleton, the internal architecture of your bones, and the soft tissue around it. From the ground, you feel an energy seeping into you, and it softly weaves itself through your body as a beautiful golden thread.

Connection

The energy moves towards your heart center. You feel the warmth that comes from your heart. It glows like a sun in your chest. Every ray is another golden thread that radiates through your body. Now you feel the golden threads that run from your heart to your head, and to your hands as they connect with the keys of your computer or the pen in your hand.

Now you feel the golden thread that runs from your heart all the way up to your throat. You feel a warm glow at your throat, and a blue light that shines out to the world from that place.

Now the golden thread runs all the way to the top of your head. Imagine it is a skylight that opens up. And from your head, shines a light that reaches all the way up to the heavens. It is your aura; it is your anchor to the universe. It is what holds you here.

Everything around you is so silent.

And as you stand on the earth, you begin to feel a rumble inside you. It is warm and powerful energy, and it moves all the way up into your throat. And before you know it, before you can question it and before you can say, 'I don't know how to...' you start to sing. And your voice is strong and singular and bright and clear. And you sing and you sing and you sing into the night sky and into the trees around you, and stars above and the moon overhead. And your voice is sturdy, and sure and it rises and rises and becomes a chorus around you. And in it you hear your pain, the strains of your laughter, the echoes of all the paths you have walked. All of it is in your singing, and you realise that everything that you need to be brave, and sure and strong in this world is captured in your voice.

Your singing breaks the silence and the stars gather closer in to listen to your stories.

Commitment

08

WHEN TO USE THIS MEDITATION

When you're struggling to finish a piece of writing or a book, when you're feeling impatient and when you feel like giving up.

The Flowing 25.5 X 36cm [watercolour and gouache]

Meditation

Get comfortable. Pull your attention inwards.

Close your eyes and rest your hands in your lap.

Check in with your breath, and let your energy slowly fall from your head. Feel all your thoughts settling like confetti and your energy sinking down.

Let your breath fill your entire chest cavity. Let it fill you all the way down to your feet as if you were filling a long thin balloon.

Then let it connect down into the earth.

Picture yourself sitting near a waterfall.

Imagine you are letting the water wash over you, and as it does, you offer up any residual beliefs about your ability to write—whether your book is valuable, whether you have talent or whether you will have readers—to the water. You feel the water cleaning away all these self-doubts, and clearing every pore of your skin, every cell of your being.

You inhale and have a sense of how much creativity and understanding and skill are flowing towards you just as the water is flowing down the side of the mountain and over you.

Not only is creativity flowing towards you, but it is pooling around you—it is not flowing away from you. It is protected. It is sacred. The earth is supporting it.

Commitment

And as you stand and receive this abundance, you feel how strongly you have invited this into your life. And you know that through the actions you're taking and the shifts in your mindsets that are happening to you as you've committed yourself to awaken the author inside you, you are inviting more creativity in your life.

You're creating space inside yourself for your book and for ideas, words, emotions, readers to come into your life. Everything you're learning here can never be lost.

Now I want you to picture a well inside your body. It can be inside your belly, your womb, your heart, anywhere you can hold energy that is flowing into you. It is your tank, your holding space for your book. And as you feel it inside your body, I want you to connect in again with why you are writing this book. Allow all the emotion, self-love, compassion and generosity that made you commit to your writing, to flow into this well inside you.

Thank the water for supporting you. From now on, every time you drink water or get into water—whether it's a bath, or a shower, or the ocean—it is a reminder to you of the creative abundance in your life, the flow that works through you.

Take another breath, and acknowledge yourself for all the learning, stretching, and work you've done. Recognize all your aha's even when it has felt hard or confusing or overwhelming. Take this moment to acknowledge how much progress you've made since you first walked into the forest, how much action you've taken, how many words you have put on the page, how far you have walked on this path.

Now send your love and appreciation to yourself for how far you've come, for how much curiosity, conviction, conscientiousness, courage, and connection you have displayed. You are developing as a writer.

Now just check in with your commitment again. What it is that you have committed to doing? Picture yourself standing up tall in your circle, and saying out loud whatever your commitment is. "I am committed to (whatever it is)."

Writing as much as I can

Getting my first draft done

Understanding the difference between plot and structure

Showing and not telling

Making time for this in my life

I am committed to not rushing, not pressuring myself, giving myself the gift of my own creativity, being courageous, finishing my book.

Now deeply thank yourself as you're learning, evolving, challenging yourself. See how much you're stretching and being stretched, and how far you've already come.

Commitment

...feel
how you
have
awoken
to your
true
power

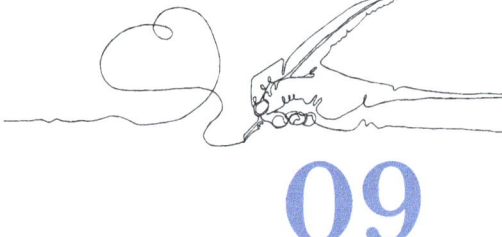

09

Chutzpah

WHEN TO USE THIS MEDITATION

When you're feeling invisible, when you're struggling to bring your story into the world, when you're afraid of the spotlight your writing will shine on you, when you need to step into the identity of a "writer" or "author" or when you need to "market" your writing and it feels scary.

Spirit 21 X 29.5cm [watercolour, digital montage]

Meditation

Close your eyes. Feel your body resting against the back of your chair, your feet firmly on the ground, your hands gently resting in your lap.

Take a few deep grounding breaths. Feel the air fill your lungs and gently exhale.

Take another breath and feel the fresh oxygen bringing life to every cell in your body. As you exhale, let go of everything you do not need to hold on to anymore.

Take a couple more deep grounding breaths.

Settle into your body.

You have come through the forest and you have reached the other side. You see the light beckoning you through the trees. And you can hear people calling your name.

And as you make your way to the end of your journey, turn and look back. Stop and breathe in all you have learned—all your conviction, curiosity, conscientiousness, courage, connection and commitment. You gather it all into your heart.

Now as you prepare to emerge from the forest, send your love and appreciation forward.

Send thanks to the editors who will work on your book, to the booksellers who will sell it, to the book cover designers who will design

your beautiful book cover, to the postmen who will be delivering your books—to all the people who will show up in your life when you need them to help you get your book out into the world.

Send your appreciation to all the readers who are going to buy your book, all those whose lives will be touched by your writing. Imagine people clicking on your book online and purchasing it. Picture people holding your book, turning the pages, crying or laughing as they read. Imagine how many people you're touching with your words. Imagine the five star reviews. Picture them.

Picture yourself sitting at your desk. Writing is now part of who you are.

This is your time. You have waited a long time for it. You have worked hard to bring your heart to the page.

Now take another few breaths and slowly open your eyes. And as you open your eyes, feel how full your heart is with the sense of what you've done and what is possible. Feel how you have awoken to your true power over the past weeks. And how everything you wish to create for yourself is waiting for you.

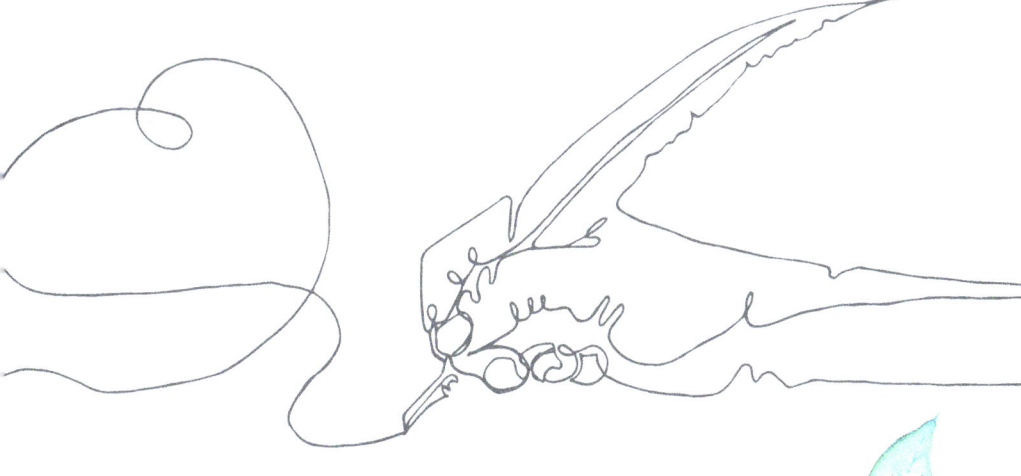

Praise

for the Author Awakening Adventure

The Author Awakening is awakening more than just the author. Blessed to be here.

—Robyn Spacey

It really was an awakening adventure. I awoke to who I really am, what I really want, how I can go about getting it and what I must develop within myself in order to succeed in completing my book. The fact that this was revealed little by little, step by step, module by module, was what made it such a delicious adventure. The course was offered by Joanne in a spirit of love, generosity and true caring. This was mirrored back by the incredible group of people sharing this journey with me.

—Bindi Davies

I cannot say enough about how the choice to do...this adventure is awakening me. It makes me realize how much I've been waiting for me to welcome this urge to write that has been with me for most of my remembered life. I know my future will be different from what it may have been two months ago. I feel so full yet only at the beginning of this journey.

—Sandra Reisinger

I don't know anybody who has had such an enormous influence on my life in such a short time. Thanks to you [Joanne], I am actually writing my story now. I know it will take a long time, but that doesn't matter. I have learned so much and you have given it to me with such graciousness and love. It takes a very special person to help so many people. I am blessed to be one of them.

—Liesbeth Bennett

Every day, I give thanks for landing here amongst it all, for Joanne. [I wish I could] articulate...how momentous this Author Awakening Adventure is. I think we will look back in years to come, realising we as yet still haven't quite grasped, that this may be the most pivotal point in our journeys so far. For healing, awakening, and moving towards the essence of who we truly are.

—Julie Balfour

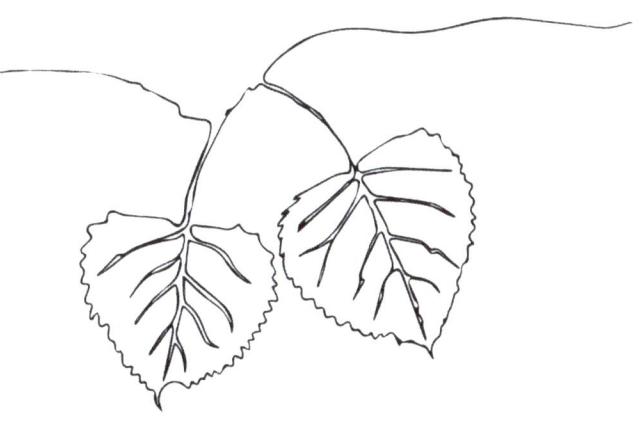

Acknowledgements

Thanks to Margaret Rolla for her beautiful illustrations and design which have brought these meditations to life through her interpretation of them in the visual form.

I am grateful to my wonderful assistant, Norie Libradilla, for the project management of this book.

I originally created these meditations for my signature eight-week course, The Author Awakening Adventure, through which more than 150 writers have passed. Their appreciation for this course and its transformational impact on them has been one of the greatest blessings of my life. This book, then, is dedicated to them and their writing.

Listen to the free audio versions of these meditations here:

www.soundcloud.com/joannefedlermedia/sets/meditations-and-visualizations-for-aspiring-authors/s-isi8X

***

If you'd like to enrol in the 8 week Author Awakening Adventure—a rollicking, life-changing, transformational course based on these qualities of consciousness, you can do so here:

www.joannefedler.com/author-awakening

About the Author

Joanne is the internationally bestselling author of ten books, including *Secret Mothers' Business, Things Without a Name, When Hungry, Eat,* and *Your Story: how to write it so others will want to read it.* Her books have been translated into many different languages and have sold close to 750 000 copies worldwide.

Born in Apartheid South Africa, she was awarded a Fulbright scholarship to study law at Yale, was a law lecturer and a volunteer legal counsellor at People Opposing Women Abuse (POWA) before setting up and running a legal advocacy center to end violence against women. She was appointed by the then Minister for Justice to sit on a project committee of the Law Commission to design new domestic violence legislation.

In 1996 Joanne was awarded a residency at Hedgebrook Women's Writer's Colony in Seattle where she began to write her first novel, *The Dreamcloth* (2005, Jacana Media). Other awards include Asshole of the Month, a title she was proud to accept from *Hustler* magazine in 1995 for her advocacy work around gender equality and the rights of all people to be free from violence.

She runs writing retreats for women all over the world and online writing courses including her signature Author Awakening Adventure and Write Your First Draft Masterclass. In 2017, she set up her own publishing company Joanne Fedler Media to publish the stories of the writers she has mentored.

Some day she hopes to set up a writer's colony, grow her own vegetables, own five cats and live in a place where she will never be stuck in traffic.

Connect with Joanne on social media or join her mailing list at: www.joannefedler.com

Or contact via e-mail at: admin@joannefedler.com

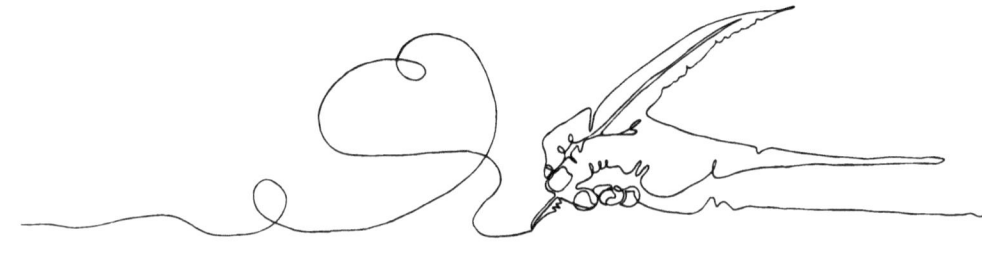